Change Has Come

Change Has Come

AN ARTIST CELEBRATES
OUR AMERICAN SPIRIT

The drawings of
KADIR NELSON

With the words of
BARACK OBAMA

SIMON & SCHUSTER BFYR

NEW YORK   LONDON   TORONTO   SYDNEY

SIMON & SCHUSTER BFYR

AN IMPRINT OF SIMON & SCHUSTER, INC.

1230 AVENUE OF THE AMERICAS, NEW YORK, NEW YORK 10020

ILLUSTRATIONS COPYRIGHT © 2009 BY KADIR NELSON

ALL RIGHTS RESERVED, INCLUDING THE RIGHT OF REPRODUCTION

IN WHOLE OR IN PART IN ANY FORM.

SIMON & SCHUSTER BFYR

IS A TRADEMARK OF SIMON & SCHUSTER, INC.

BOOK DESIGN BY LIZZY BROMLEY

THE TEXT FOR THIS BOOK IS SET IN VALERIA SCRIPT AND COCHIN.

THE ILLUSTRATIONS FOR THIS BOOK ARE RENDERED IN GRAPHITE.

MANUFACTURED IN THE UNITED STATES OF AMERICA

2 4 6 8 10 9 7 5 3 1

CIP DATA FOR THIS BOOK IS AVAILABLE FROM THE LIBRARY OF CONGRESS.

ISBN: 978-1-4169-8955-4

For

Amel, Aya, and *Ali,*

WHO FILL ME

WITH HOPE

It's the answer told by lines

that stretched aroun

chools and churches

in numbers this nation has never see

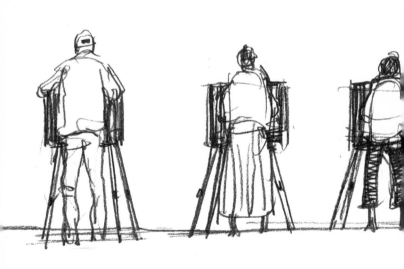

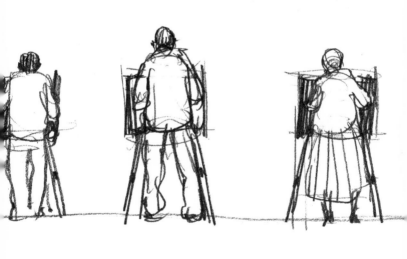

We're not going to settle anymore.

What began as a whisper has now swelle.

to a chorus that cannot be ignored.

A hymn that will heal this nation,

repair this world.

can.

In no other country

on earth,

is my story even possible.

There's not a black America

and white America

and Latino America

and Asian America.

Let us find

that common stake

we all have

in one another.

This is our moment.

This is our time.

This time

can be

different.

That is the true genius of America, a faith in the simple dreams of its people.

The audacity to hope
for what we can
and must
achieve tomorrow.

To continue the long march
of those who came before us,

a march for a more just,

more equal, more free,

more caring, and

more prosperous

America.

Together, ordinary

extraordi

people can still do

ary things.

I believe that as we stand

on the crossroads of history,

we can make the right choices,

and meet the challenges

that face us.

I promise you—

we as a people will get there.

This is your victory.

Change has come to America.

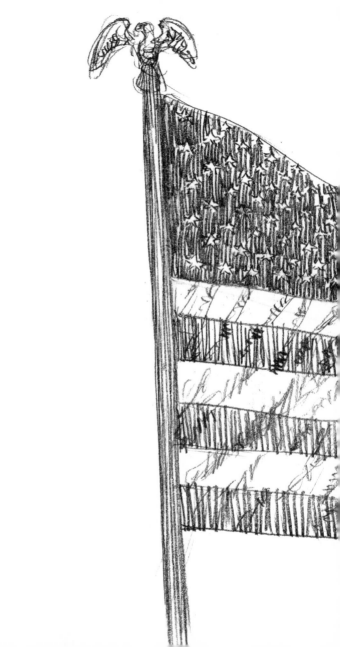

THE QUOTATIONS
WITHIN THIS BOOK ARE
Barack Obama's
OWN WORDS.

He spoke them on:

JULY 27, 2004,
during the Keynote Address at the 2004 National
Democratic Convention in Boston, Massachusetts.

JUNE 14, 2006,
in his speech at the Take Back
America Conference in Washington, DC.

FEBRUARY 5, 2008,
to a crowd of supporters on
Super Tuesday in Chicago, Illinois.

MARCH 18, 2008,
during his speech entitled "A More
Perfect Union" in Philadelphia, Pennsylvania.

NOVEMBER 4, 2008,
as he addressed the nation for the first time
as president-elect in Chicago, Illinois.

A Note from the Artist

I remember exactly where I was on election night 2008. I was in my small home studio, in the middle of working on a painting, when I learned that Barack Obama had won California to put him over the top and secure the U.S. presidency. I put down my brush and thought, *Wow, he did it. He really did it!* I ran to the television set and turned it on to see thousands of people crammed into Chicago's Grant Park, celebrating, smiling, crying, and waving signs and flags. I was instantaneously filled with a wonderful feeling. First, relief that the long campaign was finally over, and then joy. Pure joy. I felt as if I were there in the park with all of those people, celebrating and waiting to see Barack deliver his acceptance speech. And when he and his beautiful family walked out onto the stage, it was like magic. Like seeing them for the first time. Renewed and joyful. I'll never forget it. I wanted to celebrate that moment in history, and try to save a little bit of the magic that filled the air in Grant Park, and all over the country, all over the world. These very spontaneous drawings serve as a document to preserve and celebrate our great American achievement, and our new American president. I hope the artwork will remind all who see it of the greatness of our country and its ability to grow and change for the better.

I would like to extend a special thanks to my Simon & Schuster family, especially Rubin Pfeffer, whose brilliant idea for this book was both challenging and exciting; Justin Chanda, for his infectious energy and vision; and Lizzy Bromley, whose exceptional design knocked me off my feet. Thank you all for trusting me with the great task of filling the pages of this book with my artwork, and for your unwavering support and encouragement.